SIMONE BILES

GYMNASTICS SUPERSTAR

by Rachel Rose

Consultant: Beth Gambro
Reading Specialist, Yorkville, Illinois

BEARPORT
PUBLISHING

Minneapolis, Minnesota

Teaching Tips

BEFORE READING

- Look at the cover of the book. Discuss the picture and the title.

- Ask readers to brainstorm a list of what they already know about Simone Biles. What can they expect to see in this book?

- Go on a picture walk, looking through the pictures to discuss vocabulary and make predictions about the text.

DURING READING

- Read for purpose. Encourage readers to look for key pieces of information they can expect to see in biographies.

- Ask readers to look for the details of the book. What happened to Simone Biles at different times of her life?

- If readers encounter an unknown word, ask them to look at the sounds in the word. Then, ask them to look at the rest of the page. Are there any clues to help them understand?

AFTER READING

- Encourage readers to pick a buddy and reread the book together.

- Ask readers to name three things Simone Biles has done throughout her life. Go back and find the pages that tell about these things.

- Ask readers to write or draw something they learned about Simone Biles.

Credits:
Cover and title page, ©Amy Sanderson/ZUMA Wire/Alamy, Polhansen/Shutterstock, 3, ©Kathy Hutchins/Shutterstock; 5, ©Anadolu Agency/Getty Images; 7, ©Emma McIntyre / Staff/Getty Images; 8, ©Richard Ulreich/ZUMAPRESS/Newscom; 11, ©Leonard Zhukovsky/Shutterstock; 13, ©Anadolu Agency/Getty Images; 14, ©Anadolu Agency/Getty Images; 17, ©Mike Egerton/ZUMAPRESS/Newscom; 19, ©The Asahi Shimbun/Getty Images; 21, ©Taylor Hill/Contributor/Getty Images; 22, ©Salty View/Shutterstock; 23, ©imtmphoto/Shutterstock; 23, ©Salty View/Shutterstock; 23, ©Naypong Studio/Shutterstock; 23, ©SeventyFour/Shutterstock; 23, ©Sayuri Inoue/Shutterstock; 23, ©Krakenimages.com/Shutterstock

Library of Congress Cataloging-in-Publication Data

Names: Rose, Rachel, 1968- author.
Title: Simone Biles : gymnastics superstar / by Rachel Rose.
Description: Bearcub Books. | Minneapolis, Minnesota : Bearport Publishing Company, 2022. | Series: Bearcub bios | Includes bibliographical references and index.
Identifiers: LCCN 2021062572 (print) | LCCN 2021062573 (ebook) | ISBN 9781636917191 (library binding) | ISBN 9781636917269 (paperback) | ISBN 9781636917337 (ebook)
Subjects: LCSH: Biles, Simone, 1997---Juvenile literature. | Women gymnasts--United States--Biography--Juvenile literature. | Gymnasts--United States--Biography--Juvenile literature. Classification: LCC GV460.2.B55 R67 2022 (print) | LCC GV460.2.B55 (ebook) | DDC 796.44092--dc23
LC record available at https://lccn.loc.gov/2021062572
LC ebook record available at https://lccn.loc.gov/2021062573

For more information, write to Bearport Publishing, 5357 Penn Avenue South, Minneapolis, MN 55419. Printed in the United States of America.

Contents

Big Flip

Simone Biles flew high in the air.

She landed with a big smile.

Simone was very happy.

She had just finished beam at the **Olympics**.

Beam

Simone's Life

Simone was born in Ohio.

She moved to Texas when she was five.

Soon, she started living with her grandparents.

Simone calls them Mom and Dad.

Simone's Mom

Simone's Dad

Say gymnastics like jim-NAS-tiks

8

Simone fell in love with **gymnastics**.

She worked very hard.

And she was good.

Simone started winning **medals** when she was 14.

When she was 19, Simone went to the Olympics in Brazil.

She won five medals there.

And she helped her team win the gold!

Simone kept getting even better at gymnastics.

She made up really hard tricks.

Sometimes, no one else could do them!

13

When she was 24, Simone went to the Olympics in Japan.

But her tricks felt wrong.

She could not do them safely.

Simone decided not to enter all of the events.

She wanted to take care of her **mental health**.

But she cheered on her teammates.

After a few days, Simone felt she could do an event.

And she won third place.

She was very **proud** that she could do well and be safe.

Doing gymnastics changed Simone's life.

She keeps working hard at being the best she can be.

And she takes care of herself, too.

21

Did You Know?

Born: March 14, 1997

Family: Nellie (mother), Ron (father), Adria (sister), Ashley (sister), Tevin (brother), Ron Jr. (brother), Adam (brother)

When she was a kid: Doctors told her she had **ADHD**. Doing gymnastics helped her use up her energy.

Special fact: Simone loves dogs. She has two of them. They are called Lilo and Rambo.

Simone says: "Dreams do come true."

Life Connections

Simone believes in taking care of herself. She works hard and she lets herself rest, too. Was there a time when taking a break was the best thing for you to do?

Glossary

ADHD something that can make it hard to pay attention

gymnastics a sport made up of tumbling and flipping

medals shiny awards given to winners in sports

mental health to do with the wellness of a person's mind

Olympics a world sports contest held every four years

proud very happy because of something you have done

Index

Read More

Fishman, Jon M. *Gymnastics Superstar: Simone Biles (Bumba Books—Sports Superstars).* Minneapolis: Lerner Publications, 2019.

Moening, Kate. *Simone Biles: Olympic Gymnast (Women Leading the Way).* Minneapolis: Bellwether Media, 2020.

Learn More Online

1. Go to **www.factsurfer.com** or scan the QR code below.
2. Enter "**Simone Biles**" into the search box.
3. Click on the cover of this book to see a list of websites.

About the Author

Rachel Rose is a writer. When she was young, she and her sister won a school gymnastics competition.